The Chinese Triads: The History and Legacy of China's Most Organized Crime Syndicates

By Charles River Editors

About Charles River Editors

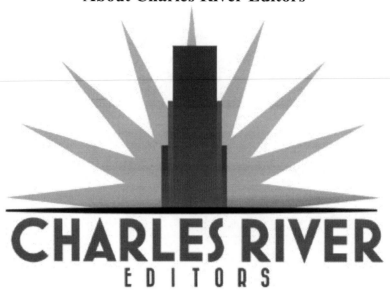

Charles River Editors is a boutique digital publishing company, specializing in bringing history back to life with educational and engaging books on a wide range of topics. Keep up to date with our new and free offerings with this 5 second sign up on our weekly mailing list, and visit Our Kindle Author Page to see other recently published Kindle titles.

We make these books for you and always want to know our readers' opinions, so we encourage you to leave reviews and look forward to publishing new and exciting titles each week.

Introduction

From running guns to white-collar crimes in cyberspace and illegal seafood, the Triads, the mafia of China, are potent figures in the world of organized crime. Going by enigmatic names like the 14K Triad and the United Bamboo Gang, these criminal groups are enormous, with some organizations boosting memberships ranging in the tens of thousands. A powerful factor in China and throughout Asia, Triads are entrenched in society and the masters of multiple enterprises ranging from extortion, narcotics, prostitution and white collar crime.

Despite their origins in mainland China, the Triads are most powerful in Hong Kong and Taiwan; as an international organization, the Triads have expanded into North America and other Western countries. The various Triad organizations are different but share many similarities, including a hierarchical structure, exclusive membership, common commercial money-making activities, the use of violence as a tool and the codification of rituals for the group. Although the various Triad groups share a common Chinese ethnic origin, these groups are fiercely territorial and do not collaborate together too often.

The modern Triads trace their lineage to a group called the Hung Mun (Heaven and Earth Association). Originating in the Qing Dynasty as a secret society focused on Han solidarity and the restoration of the Ming Dynasty, these groups sought to overthrow the foreign Manchu Qing rulers. The Hung Mun positioned themselves as self-help organizations to disfranchised Chinese workers, providing them money loans and welfare when they were ignored by the government.

From these secretive anti-Qing groups to their current existence as powerful organized crime groups, the Triads have continued to evolve and grow. Taking full advantage of technological changes, the Triads have become major players in cybercrime and the illegal seafood trade, forcing law enforcement to evolve in order to combat them.

The Chinese Triads: The History and Legacy of China's Most Famous Organized Crime Syndicates explores the organizations' origins and their inner workings.

The Origins of the Triad Gangs

The historical origins of the Chinese Triads can be traced to lineage among the secret societies that festered alongside the imperial dynasties. In the history of China, the overthrow of each dynasty and the succeeding ruler was "justified by the assumption that heaven smiled on a good ruler and protected him while it foiled a poor one and eventually provided for his overthrow."[1] A huge part of this ideological heritage is intimately tied to organized crime, a tradition that spans hundreds of years. These societies were called Triads and were originally patriotic resistance movements of ethnic Chinese started in opposition to the non-Chinese Manchu rulers of the last Chinese dynasty, the Qing, who overthrew the Han Chinese Ming Dynasty in 1644.[2]

The word Triad was actually coined by the British who ruled Hong Kong as a colony. It was a reference to the triangular shape of the Chinese character for "secret society." The character was shaped to symbolize the unity of heaven, earth, man and represented the quasi-religious nature of these secret societies.[3] These secret societies during the Qing were passionate zealots that believed in the Ming "as a bygone golden age."[4]

One of the self-described myths among the Chinese Triads themselves is their ancestral connection to a group of warrior monks. The Qing Dynasty ruled during a time where they were under constant threat from external enemies. As a result, the imperial armies were perpetually repelling military invasions. Seeking more capable fighters for his armies, the Emperor K'ang Hsi, sought volunteers from a group of legendary warrior monks at the Siu Lam monastery in Fujian Province.[5] The monks were expert fighters, skilled in martial arts and combat. Joining the imperial armies, they became integral in defeating the invading foreign forces. However, after they completed their mission, the monks refused their rewards. Instead, they returned to the monastery. The Emperor and his advisors realized that these monks were a potential powerful threat to imperial rule. To counter this threat, the Emperor mustered an army to eliminate the monks.

However, these monks were highly skilled warriors and the imperial Qing troops were aware of their superior military skills. Because of this, the imperial troops believed they needed the element of surprise to defeat the powerful monks. But the Qing forces had an ace up their sleeve. Imperial generals attacked with the assistance of an expelled renegade monk, Ma Yee Fuk, who provided intelligence on escape tunnels.[6] With their inside source, the Qing attack was successful

---

[1] Sharon Tracy, *The Evolution of the Hong Kong Triads/Tongs into the Current Drug Market* (Journal of Third World Studies, vol. 10, no. 1, 1993), 22.

[2] Tracy, 22.

[3] Jennifer Bolz, *Chinese Organized Crime and Illegal Alien Trafficking: Humans as a Commodity* (Asian Affairs, vol. 22, no. 3, 1995), 148.

[4] Tracy, 22.

[5] Tracy, 23.

[6] Tracy, 24.

and the monastery was burned to the ground. Eighteen monks managed to escape, but that number quickly dwindled to five as the rest died of disease and injuries. Bitter from their downfall, the surviving five monks vowed to avenge their fallen monks and to overthrow the Qing Dynasty.

Finding refuge in a monastery in Guangdong province, the monks were introduced to five Ming Dynasty officials, now rebel leaders. Together the men allied in a joint effort to defeat the Qing. The monks established a headquarters and started to recruit and organize new members. Forming a secret society, they adopted clandestine recognition signals and communication codes and oaths of loyalty.[7] As time passed, the secret society realized they could achieve their goals more effectively by dividing the Qing Dynasty's attention. Five separate groups were spread throughout China. The second of these groups would head to the southern Chinese province of Guangdong which would become a major center of power for the modern Triads.

This movement became known as the Action of the Triad and initiated several rebellions during the eighteenth and nineteenth centuries. However, the Triads were already deeply involved in many criminal activities, as stated by this statement of their activity in 1890:

Their members would stop at nothing to unlawfully monopolize, extort and blackmail, criminally embezzle and deprive, bully and oppress people, disrupt commerce, engage in larceny and robbery, kidnap, traffic in drugs, operate casinos or bawdy houses or drug saloons, smuggle, traffic in weaponry, murder, abduct, or commit any other crime imaginable.[8]

Qing rule ended in 1911, defeated by the Nationalist Republic of China founded by Dr. Sun Yat-sen. The Triads group did not disband, instead continuing and morphing into fully functioning criminal societies. Dr. Sun Yat Sen himself was supported by the Triads.[9] But before the overthrow of the Qing, the Triads movement still maintained a primary mission that was politically motivated. But with that mission accomplished, the large number of criminals in the Triad groups did not wish to give up their enterprises just because the political mission had been accomplished.[10] Even in the early stages of the Triad development as a full-fledged criminal enterprise, their influence was already immense. For example, Wang Jinrong, the boss of the Ching Gang was the Inspector General of the Police in the French Concession in Shanghai.[11] General Chiang Kai-Shek, leader of the Nationalist Republic, used Wang and his Triad connections for support while ruling. According to the Enterprise Crime Conference:

Aside from the number one boss, Wang Jinrong, the other bosses held the high post in the KMT army and the municipal or provincial government - all these bosses formed the gang's

---

[7] Tracy, 24.
[8] Tracy, 25.
[9] Tracy, 25.
[10] Tracy, 25.
[11] Tracy, 26.

leader-ship and monopolized the gang's decision-making, leaving intermediate important positions to their "disciples" under the camouflage of such titles as "Director General," "General Manager," "Trustee of Chamber of Commerce," etc., taking care of various ad hoc criminal activities, and entrusting their underlings with specific assignments to execute (give orders or organize) a particular crime, with those at the bottom - hooligans, hitters, killers and other specialized criminals - to carry out the actual criminal activities.[12]

As mainland China fell under Communist control, Hong Kong became the major epicenter for Triad activity. Hong Kong under British control was already a valuable port city for the opium trade. This factor helped change the Triads from a political organization to its eventual modern existence as full-fledged criminal powerhouses. The Triads grew in strength in Hong Kong during the nineteenth and twentieth centuries where they were seen as a major threat to both the Qing and the later British colonial rulers. This increased suppression further drove the Triads underground, morphing them into Hak She Wui (Black Society), an organization which operated various criminal activities.[13]

The Communist Chinese who ascended into power in China during the late 1940s sought to eliminate Triads in mainland China. The communists were ruthless in their purge of the criminals. Countless drug dealers were thrown into prison, where many of them were executed quickly with pistols. While the Communist Revolution of China succeeded in ridding mainland China of its opium problem, the Triads were able to escape despite the relentless purge. Many gangsters fled to Taiwan with Chiang's Nationalist army while others fled to Hong Kong. Finally, some fled into Southeast Asia, particularly the area known as the Golden Triangle (famous for its heroin production).

But some Triad groups continued their connection to political activities which they used to both "disguise and justify the pursuit of illicit profits."[14] This is demonstrated by Tao Siju in 1992, the Minister of Public Security in China, stating, "lauded the patriotic work of some triads and welcomed them to set up business in China—comments that coincided with investments in mainland China planned by Sun Yee On triad."[15] The Mainland Chinese government utilized a "united front" approach to engage the more "patriotic" Triad members and groups in order to ensure both Hong Kong's prosperity, stability and to defend against penetration of Taiwanese based Triads such as the United Bamboo Gang and the Four Seas.[16] The Beijing mainland government was especially concerned about these Taiwan based groups which were possibly connected to anti-Beijing groups, pro-democratic Triads that were counter to the communist Chinese regime. Triads had previously influenced local elections and caused violence in Macau, a Portuguese colony in China and Beijing wanted control of these groups to avoid these incidents

---

[12] Tracy, 26.

[13] Broadhurst and Lee, 10.

[14] Broadhurst and Lee, 10.

[15] Broadhurst and Lee, 10.

[16] Broadhurst and Lee, 10.

from occurring.

Triad Organization

Triad members are usually linked by language and their lineage to their ancestral villages. Through secret rituals of oath of allegiance, enforced by fear of death, members were expected to place absolute faith in the organization. Membership in the Triad ensured a high level of political and economic connections.[17] Triads also partner with local youth gangs along with legitimate businesses and government associations.

Triads have a mysterious and secretive system of numeric codes to identify ranks and positions within the gangs. Many of these numbers are inspired by the I Ching, an ancient Chinese of philosophy and numerology. Traditionally, the top of the Triad hierarchy is the Dragon Master or Dragon Head. The Dragon's Head proxy, the Incense Master is in charge of the induction ceremony for the Triads. The Incense Master's lieutenant is the Vanguard. The title Red Pole is granted to the military commander of the Triad group who oversees the offensive and defensive operations of the group. The White Paper Fan is the finance and business leader and the Straw Sandal acts as the liaison between the different factions. Finally, the title Blue Lantern is granted to uninitiated members which are similar to "non-made" men in the American Italian mafia. An important fact to remember about these traditional ranking systems is that the Triads have undergone a great deal of change in the last few decades, particularly since the 21st century. Law enforcement now believe that many of these traditional ranks are no longer as common as they were in the past.

According to a U.S. Senate report, "Triad membership is thus a valuable asset to the new international criminal. Triad membership facilitates criminal activities in a manner similar to the way membership in business associations facilitates the activities of a legitimate businessman."[18]

Triads are exceedingly difficult organizations to penetrate for law enforcement due to their membership makeup based on "strong filial and geographic loyalties."[19] Due to their intricate global networks, Triads are both reactive and flexible organizations capable of countering law enforcement. Triads are simultaneously highly organized and decentralized. Although Triads are hierarchical organizations, commands are not always disseminated from the top down.[20] Both members and affiliates are given a high degree of flexibility and freedom to conduct their own criminal operations. This unusual freedom is illustrated by the testimony of a Hong Kong Triad member to a Senate subcommittee in 1992:

I was not required to pay any percentage of profits to the 14K leadership. Triads do not work

---

[17] Bolz, 148.
[18] Bolz, 148.
[19] Bolz, 153.
[20] Bolz, 153.

that way. Triad members do favors for each other, provide introductions and assistance to each other, engage in criminal schemes with one another, but tri-ads generally do not have the kind of strictly disciplined organizational structure that other criminal groups like the Italian mafia.[21]

In the event that a Triad member is arrested, this decentralization and cross-membership of the Triads assists the gangsters from potentially giving too much pertinent information. In the event that a Triad gangster reveals the general structure of his network (even specific information like the names and addresses of senior gangsters), the group can still survive. Direct links between the various Triad members and affiliates are difficult to connect. For instance, a Big Circle member "testified that he was the leader of a subordinate gang within the Big Circle called the 'Flaming Eagles.' He also was a member of the Wo On Lok Triad, a subsidiary of the Wo Group in Hong Kong."[22]

There are seven major Triad organizations: Sun Yee On Triad, Wo Group, 14K Triad, Luen Group, Big Circle Gang, United Bamboo Gang, and The Four Seas Gang. Not all of these groups adhere to the quasi-religious organizational structure of the Triads. But all these groups do conduct criminal enterprises through a network of international connections, with larger groups coordinating the operations of multiple subordinate groups under direct control or through proxies.[23]

List of Chinese Triad Groups[24]

Sun Yee On Triad (Hong Kong)

- Largest Hong Kong-based Triad

- 25,000 plus members

- 2,000 plus office bearers

- Affiliated associates in New York City, Los Angeles, Canada, Australia and Thailand

Wo Group (Hong Kong)

- 20,000 plus members within ten subgroups

- Wo Shing Wo Triad is largest subgroup

- Wo Hop To Triad has a major base of operations in San Francisco

---

[21] Bolz, 153.
[22] Bolz, 153.
[23] Bolz, 148.
[24] Bolz, 155-156.

14K Triad (Hong Kong)

- 20,000 plus members

- Over thirty subgroups

- Leadership is dispersed

- Associates in America, Canada, Australia and throughout Asia

Luen Group (Hong Kong)

- 8,000 plus members in four subgroups

- Luen Kung Lok Triad has a presence in North America, particularly Toronto

Big Circle Gang (Mainland China, Hong Kong)

- Established by former Communist Red Guards who fled to Hong Kong

- Most members are also Triad members

- Has active cells around the world, especially in Hong Kong, Canada and New York City

United Bamboo Gang (Taiwan)

- Biggest Taiwan based group

- 20,000 plus members

- Operations in New York, Los Angeles and Houston

Four Seas Gang (Taiwan)

- 5,000 plus members

- Operations in Los Angeles

Chinese Triads based in Hong Kong are some of the largest and most powerful organized criminal groups in the world.[25] Their operations include a combination of illegal activities such as gambling, prostitution, heroin trade, human trafficking and gambling along with legitimate businesses. Some Hong Kong factions are highly disciplined and organized, with members

---

[25] Sheldon Zhang and Ko-lin Chin, *The Declining Significance of Triad Societies in Transnational Illegal Activities: A Structural Deficiency Perspective* (The British Journal of Criminology, vol. 43, no. 3, 2003), 471.

becoming influential figures in Hong Kong.[26] Being international organizations, Hong Kong-based groups are also heavily involved in mainland China, North America and Southeast Asia.

A second major center for Triad power in Asia is Taiwan. The origins of the Taiwanese based Triad groups can be traced to Mainland China's recovery of Taiwan from Japan after it was a Japanese colony. Taiwan Triads conduct many traditional criminal operations including gambling dens, prostitution, and extortion. But they are also heavily entrenched in the legitimate businesses in Taiwan. Gang members own restaurants, cafes, clubs, movies, cable television, magazine and construction companies.[27] Taiwanese Triads are also involved in white collar crime like futures trading, and stock and commercial activities, including "collusive bidding for government projects."[28]

But the Triads are an international criminal organization and operate in countries outside of China, Taiwan and Hong Kong. Triads operate in many countries with Chinese migrants and Chinese migration has been a historic trend. Throughout history, China has consistently experienced a series of chaotic political, economic and sociological conflicts that drove a constant stream of Chinese migrants out of China.[29] The first migrations of Chinese were exclusive to other Asian countries (Southeast Asia). However, as trade continued to expand throughout the world, Chinese people started immigrating to areas outside of Asia. Upon arriving in these new areas, the Chinese formed tight knit communities where most residents did not speak a non-Chinese language and remained segregated culturally from the area.

Triad groups have been particularly active in North America. The first Chinese Triad groups were established in San Francisco in the 1850s during the initial wave of Chinese immigration. Chinese crime groups are known as Tongs in America. The word "Tong" means "hall" or "place." [30] Prior to the establishment of Tongs in American Chinatowns, the Chinese communities were ruled by a either a dominant family or several associations. Many of the Chinese migrants were left out of these organizations and formed their own associations called Tongs. As there were no special restrictions on what qualified a Tong, unlike the previous associations which were strict about its members belonging to one family or village, Tongs were able to spread rapidly throughout the Chinatowns of America, with over 30 groups in various cities.[31] These Tongs often battled each other for control of territory.

The Tongs in these Chinatowns provided many valuable services such as job referrals and housing assistance. These organizations were the only reliable source of these important services for many Chinese immigrants who were barred legally and culturally from other avenues. The

---

[26] Zhang and Chin, 471.
[27] Zhang and Chin, 471.
[28] Zhang and Chin, 471.
[29] Tracy, 30.
[30] Zhang and Chin, 472.
[31] Zhang and Chin, 472.

Tongs also acted as mediators between both group and individual conflicts within the Chinatown community.[32] Many Tong members operate legally with their own businesses or legal jobs. These members interact with the associations by paying a fee and meeting at the Tong with other members for social gatherings and Tongs often hold banquets and picnics throughout the year. Leaders of the Tongs can wield much influence in the lives of their group members, controlling even their daily affairs and they also usually have relationships with youth street gangs, using them as soldiers for criminal operations. Tongs have been active in opium smuggling, gambling, brothels as well as narcotics and human trafficking.[33] Tongs are considered by American law enforcement to be organized crime groups that conduct transnational crime and in the 1990s, several Tongs in San Francisco, New York, Chicago, Houston and Atlanta were indicted as racketeering organizations.[34]

Finally, there are the Chinese American street gangs. In the 1990s, there were more Chinese street gangs in New York City than any other American city, making New York the epicenter of Chinese organized crime in America.[35] The first Chinese street gang, known as the Continentals, was formed in 1961. Formed by high school students, these Chinese youths established the gang as a means of self-protection. Over the years, other Chinese gangs were created: the White Eagles, Black Eagles, Ghost Shadows and Flying Dragons. In the early years of these gangs, they were mostly martial arts clubs led by a master who was also a Tong member. These gangs transformed themselves in the late 1960s and early 1970s, becoming predatory criminal groups rather than entities that aided the community. They harassed and terrorized the Chinese community by extorting local businesses and robbed gambling establishments.[36] However, because businesses extorted by these youth gangs were Tong members, many Tongs started to hire other gang members as protection to defend against rival gangs. These alliances further solidified the position of these gangs in the Chinese Chinatown community.

In the 1980s, several new street gangs such as Fuk China, White Tigers, Tung On, Green Dragons, Golden Star and Born-to-Kill all emerged in New York's Chinatown, Queens and Brooklyn.[37] This huge uptick in gang activity was the result of renewed Chinese immigration and businesses. Chinese gangs also spread to cities outside the major urban Chinatowns, such as Oakland, Houston, Falls Church, Arlington, Philadelphia, Chicago and Boston.[38] American law enforcement started to classify Chinese street gangs as organized crime and by the 1990s all major Asian street gangs had been indicted as racketeering enterprises.[39]

Triad Customs

---

[32] Zhang and Chin, 472.
[33] Zhang and Chin, 472.
[34] Zhang and Chin, 472.
[35] Zhang and Chin, 472.
[36] Zhang and Chin, 472.
[37] Zhang and Chin, 472.
[38] Zhang and Chin, 472.
[39] Zhang and Chin, 472.

As a secret society, the Triads have many formal initiation ceremonies and rituals and these elaborate rituals separated the Triads from their contemporaries. Although the various Triad groups used different distinct ceremonies, all of these rituals are similar enough to be classified under the same system.

Many of the rituals adopted by the Qing Dynasty Triads were not distinct only to the Triads. In fact, many oaths, ceremonies and rituals were developed from folk religions, oral traditions and novels (such as the famous *Romance of the Three Kingdoms*).[40] For instance, oaths often contained venerations of Heaven as the father and Earth as the mother ("Obedient to Heaven in preparing the Way").[41] This use of popular and well known stories and slogans from culture was a useful recruiting method since even the average person joining the Triad would have heard about such infamous tales.

The key distinguishing feature of the Triads groups was their secretive initiation ceremonies. These involved blood oaths, often at night in deserted temples or secluded areas, and were intense and solemn affairs. For example, in an 1802 Triad ceremony in Xiangshan, an altar was erected that displayed "five multi-colored flags, a mirror, a sword, and a pair of scissors."[42] A yellow piece of paper, the names and ages of each pledge was written, with an oath that states: "Willingly we take the surname of Hong, and worship Heaven as our father, and Earth as our mother; if there are calamities, our [sworn] brothers will lend us support; but if we betray this oath, we shall perish by the sword."[43] Afterwards, the Triad pledges burned the paper oath and sipped liquor mixed with blood.

Other Triad ceremonies include pledges passing under a drawn sword or several blades while a senior Triad member uttered the oath. This ceremony was known as "crossing the bridge."[44] Some Triad ceremonies had recruits kneeling before a senior member while taking the oath. These oaths became more elaborate in their complexity as the Triads developed. By the nineteenth century, Triad initiation ceremonies included the exaltation of the "Five Ancestors" and the "Thirty-Six Oaths."[45] New recruits learned their group's secret codes and sign languages, a key component of identifying other brothers. ("If a member happens to be in company, and wishes to discover whether there be a brother present, he takes up his tea-cup . . . with the thumb, the fore, and middle fingers, or with the fore, middle, and third fingers, and which, if perceived by an initiated person is answered by a corresponding sign.")[46] These codes and signals were used by members to test strangers in order to ascertain whether they belonged to the same group.

---

[40] Robert J. Antony, *The Structures of Crime*, (Unruly People: Crime, Community, and State in Late Imperial South China, 1st ed., Hong Kong University Press, Hong Kong, 2016), 109.
[41] Antony, 109.
[42] Antony, 110.
[43] Antony, 110.
[44] Antony, 110.
[45] Antony, 110.
[46] Antony, 110.

The phrases were designed to be confusing and cryptic. Written materials were also used by these early Triad groups although many of them have since been lost.

In Triad philosophy, the criminal acts and violence conducted by their groups were justified by their connection to *jiang hu*, "which allows a life outside normal social customs and obligations."[47] These were organizations that operated by intense rituals of loyalty and secrecy, tracing its lineage to the mythology of the secretive patriotic groups that had codes of conduct that guided the behavior of each Triad member. Entry to the Triad composed strict fealties of loyalty that created a sworn brotherhood that was "devoid of class distinctions, favoritism, or hatred among brothers."[48] A Triad's traditional code authorized violence according to their unique code, including: in the pursuit of revenge, honor, violation of that code and legitimized violence done in the name of their criminal endeavors.

An important cultural element of Chinese culture is "guan xi" (interpersonal reciprocity) and this component is also extremely important within the Triads.[49] Guan xi is used to create trust and interpersonal networks. This basis of exchange centered on personal obligation is key to the "patron-client" relationship within Triad organizations. The Dai lo (big brother) is the center in these networked personal relationships.[50] Hong Kong being an immigrant city, the Triads provided both social capital in the absence of family and joining the Triad offered individuals protection from exclusion and unemployment.

Hong Kong and the Triads

Hong Kong has been the power center for the Triad groups for centuries. A world class economic city, the former British colony has not always been powerful on the international stage. When the British first arrived in 1841, Hong Kong was a sleepy fishing town with a population that totaled less than 10,000 people.[51]

Situated in the southern Guangdong province of China, Hong Kong was in an area covered by the Triads. This was evidenced by the passage of anti-Triad laws in 1844. Escaping these laws, Triads started to operate under the guise of workers guilds and associations. Many Chinese also did not trust the British government at the time which turned many people to the Triads for assistance. The Triads utilized this to further solidify their power and growth[52] and the Triads were very effective at controlling their legal and illegal operations. However, Triads were also constantly splintering and fighting each other, with members constantly leaving to protect themselves, only to end up forming other Triad groups themselves.[53]

---

[47] Broadhurst and Lee, 10.
[48] Broadhurst and Lee, 10.
[49] Broadhurst and Lee, 12.
[50] Broadhurst and Lee, 12.
[51] Tracy, 27.
[52] Tracy, 27.
[53] Tracy, 28.

In the first half of the century, about 300 different Triad groups operated in Hong Kong and during the Second World War, some Triad groups even collaborated with the Japanese. When Hong Kong fell to the Japanese in the war, the Japanese reformed the cooperative Triads into an organization called the Hing Ah Kee Kwan (The Asia Flourishing Society).[54] The Japanese authorities used these groups to help keep order in Hong Kong. The Triads benefited from this alliance because the Japanese gave them control of the opium trade and other profits from prostitution and gambling. Because of these connections, the collaborative Triad groups gained tremendous power in narcotics trafficking, gambling and prostitution after the war.[55]

When the Nationalist Chinese government was defeated in 1949 by the Communists in the civil war, thousands of refugees fled from mainland China to Taiwan, Hong Kong and other Asian countries. Many of these refugees were Triad members. The British, who had regained control of Hong Kong, viewed these Triads as helpful to maintaining stability among the thousands of mainland Chinese refugees in the city.[56] But the British also banned opium in Hong Kong and this move reintroduced an exploding black market, giving the Triads increased income and power.

It was in the post war period that the Hong Kong Triads began playing an even bigger role in the international narcotics trade. By the 1950s, the power struggles and infighting among the Hong Kong Triads had caused major disturbances in the city. British law enforcement countered these actions by detaining over 10,000 suspected Triad members during the October 10, 1956 riot in Kowloon and deported over 600 members.[57] Several Triad groups were weakened because of these actions, some never recovering and many guilds and associations that served as front groups for the Triads were shuttered. The Triads that survived adapted by maintaining a low profile.

But the Triads emerged publicly again in Hong Kong in the summer of 1967 due to a series of unrest and riots.[58] The underground Triad groups had taken advantage of the relative economic prosperity and increased their control over the illegal activities of drugs, prostitution and gambling.[59]

The modern Triads continue to be formidable opponents of law enforcement in Hong Kong. In the 1990s, as many as 50 Triad groups operated in Hong Kong. These groups varied from several hundred members to tens of thousands of members like the mighty San Yee On. Hong Kong Triads remain heavily involved in their traditional activities, such as gambling, extortion and loansharking and Triad members operate in the organization depending on their age, motivation

---

[54] Tracy, 28.
[55] Tracy, 28.
[56] Tracy, 28.
[57] Tracy, 28.
[58] Tracy, 29.
[59] Tracy, 29.

and ability.[60] A great deal of modern Triad activity in Hong Kong actually revolves around the youth street gangs. These youth gangs consist mostly of young men between the ages of 12 to 18 years old and youths often join these gangs for a sense of identity. Once in the gang, many start dressing alike, aligning themselves with the same brand of clothing, cigarettes and socializing in one or two favorite locations (a "home base").[61] While some of these youth gang members represented the traditional Triads, most members held no real loyalty to the Triad and often left the gangs once they reached adulthood, either because of school or employment.

However, some gang members "graduated" from the youth gangs, becoming criminals in the Triad. Starting at 16 to 25 years old, the majority of these individuals would become full-fledged members of Triad society (leaders, Triad officeholders). These members did not usually have regular jobs, instead operating street-level activities such as: "extortion of shopkeepers, protection of businesses, debt collection, pimping for prostitutes, and the sale and distribution of drugs."[62] While some Hong Kong criminal groups featured members from a single Triad, some groups also included members from various Triads, but all of these members resorted to violence as a tool.

One of the major elements of the Hong Kong Triad's power comes from the city's proximity to the heroin producing area of the Golden Triangle. The Golden Triangle is located in a region where the borders of Burma, Laos and Thailand intersect. This area, roughly the size of England, is controlled by several warlords and tribes.[63] The heroin poppies are grown by the members of the various hill tribes–the Shan, the Hmong, the Wa and the Akha, who are skilled at navigating the dense and treacherous terrain.[64] In this lawless region, opium is produced, refined and smuggled throughout the world by the Hong Kong Triads.

Using the heroin grown in the Golden Triangle, the Triads are responsible for most of the heroin grown in these areas of Southeast Asia into the United States, Australia, Malaysia, Taiwan, Thailand, Singapore and Hong Kong itself.[65] Often, Chinese nationals are used to transport heroin into America using commercial marine vessels, air freight, mail parcels and commercial air flights.

Smuggling

Another key component of Triad activity internationally are its human smuggling operations.

Although the general western public is only aware of Asian human smuggling when it ends in tragedy, such as the death of 58 illegal Chinese immigrants inside a refrigerator truck in Dover,

---

[60] Tracy, 29.
[61] Tracy, 29.
[62] Tracy, 30.
[63] Tracy, 30.
[64] Tracy, 30.
[65] Tracy, 30.

England in 2000.[66] These operations have only continued to increase as the economic and commercial growth, technology and ease of travel expands the reach of organized crime groups like the Triads.

Human smugglers in the Triad are known as "snakeheads" and these smuggling operations are so successful that they are considered a threat to legal immigration by law enforcement officials. Snakeheads use several methods and routes to smuggle people into America. One strategy is to travel to Mexico or Canada and attempt to cross the border.[67] Another strategy is to fly into America via multiple transit points outside China although these illegal migrants would still need documents to enter America once they land. A third strategy is to smuggle large groups of people by freighters and fishing trawlers.

There are two types of snakeheads within the Triads–big snakeheads and little snakeheads. Big snakeheads invest the money and supervise the smuggling operations. These individuals are often overseas Chinese and usually do not know the people that are being smuggled. Big snakeheads are often wealthy businessmen and have great power and connections. Little snakeheads, on the other hand, work as middlemen and recruiters.[68] These individuals usually live in communities in China that are responsible for sending people and they also collect payments.

In recent years, powerful Triad groups have increasingly overtaken illegal immigrant smuggling operations from smaller organizations. A key factor to this change is that unlike drug trafficking, human smuggling ensures huge profits without the potential of the severe legal penalties of narcotics smuggling.[69] For instance, although profits from illegal human smuggling is estimated by authorities to total 3.2 billion dollars per year, the crime is only punishable by five years in jail (most smugglers convicted only sentenced to less than six months).[70]

Trips from China to America or Europe can take up to two years and cost upwards of $35,000. If an individual wants to fly into America with forged documents, the price increases to $45,000. This is a high price tag to pay for the average Chinese person. American law enforcement authorities estimate about 50 percent to two-thirds "of this price is dividends high by cutting back on overhead journeys are often unseaworthy, and the crowded squalor."[71]

These illegal immigrants were mostly men who often did not pay the complete cost of their journey until years after they arrived at their destinations. To leave China, illegal migrants paid a down payment to their snakeheads ranging from $100 to the entire amount (the amount paid

---

[66] Zhang and Chin, 474.
[67] Zhang and Chin, 474.
[68] Zhang and Chin, 474.
[69] Bolz, 148.
[70] Bolz, 148.
[71] Bolz, 148.

often depended on the financial situation of the family).[72] The rest of the amount would be paid in the destination country. Upon arriving, illegal migrants were forced to work in sweatshops or other illegal activities such as drug or currency trafficking in order to pay back their transit amount. Failing to do so could be disastrous. Snakeheads would violently attack the illegal migrants or their families in China if payment was not received.

Triads organize mass human smuggling operations through various travel agencies controlled by the crime groups. These agencies would then plan the routes and the logistics for the smuggling activities. China's Public Security Bureau estimates around several hundred thousand Chinese all over the world (Russia, Bangkok, Saigon, Africa, Latin America and Europe) travel using these agencies.[73] Triad groups often used highly creative methods to obtain their goals. For example, Triad leaders in Spain had a clever ruse for human smuggling. Identification papers of legal citizens are reused when the individual died so that the official Spanish government population of Chinese migrants never changed, leaving the authorities ignorant.[74]

Although Triad groups smuggle internationally, the traditional center of these operations are centered in Hong Kong. But in recent years, Taiwan based Triad groups have rapidly increased their human smuggling operations, becoming the new epicenter for these activities in Asia. According to Willard H. Myers III, an Asian crime expert, Taiwanese Triad groups now "represent the most powerful group in transnational ethnic Chinese organized crime...and are in total control of the global transportation networks whether by air or sea."[75] The American Immigration and Naturalization Service states: "The boats are set up there, the money is laundered there. The behind-the-scenes people who control some of the gangs that pick up at airports, control safe houses, and collect money are also Taiwanese."[76]

This increased Taiwanese Triad influence has often reared its head in shockingly violent incidents, exploding into mainstream society. In 1984, San Francisco journalist Henry Liu was murdered by members of the powerful Taiwanese United Bamboo Union after writing a critical biography of Chiang Ching-Kuo, the former president of Taiwan. According to a U.S. Senate report, the Taiwanese Defense Intelligence Bureau personally requested the United Bamboo Union to conduct the assassination.[77] Although shocking, this connection between the Taiwanese Triads and the Taiwan government was not unusual. Historically, the many elements of the Taiwanese government, including its intelligence agencies have been complicit in organized crime operations. Myers again notes: "Wherever the Taiwanese government has made significant loans or grants and wherever large-scale investment has been made in establishing export oriented industrial facilities, the smuggling of people and commodities had followed."[78]

---

[72] Bolz, 148.
[73] Bolz, 149.
[74] Bolz, 149.
[75] Bolz, 149.
[76] Bolz, 149.
[77] Bolz, 149.

Taiwanese Triads use various countries around the world for its smuggling operations. In recent decades, Guatemala has become a key staging ground for many large Triad smuggling activities. Taiwanese nationals in Guatemala coordinate the smuggling operations with those in Southern California, making the Central American country a major staging area. Taiwanese Triads also have connections in Belize, Dominican Republic, Jamaica and Puerto Rico.[79]

However, the nature of human trafficking has changed in recent years. Many experts now believe that although the Triads remain involved in smuggling activities, non-Triad members are increasing their participation. Most of these individuals have no Triad affiliations at all, rather private businessmen with a flair and ability to smuggle illegal migrants. Armed with their own connections and networks which provide them both the methods and routes, they are able to operate without Triad assistance. For instance, in 1994, American authorities arrested 18 Chinese in New York for human smuggling. All of these smugglers belonged to one of five smuggling rings, with several belonging to more than one group.[80] This trend seems to have also affected narcotics trafficking. Logic dictates that organized crime groups possess the manpower, connections and operational capabilities to transport drugs and material across multiple international borders. But law enforcement is increasingly realizing that the reality is much different than they had previously assumed. As stated by one high ranking Hong Kong police official:

There is a commonly held misconception that the illegal drug trade in Hong Kong and in other countries with Hong Kong Chinese involvement, is monopolized by Hong Kong triads. This makes sensational news but is simply not true. Triad membership is not a prerequisite for joining a drug syndicate; it is experience, expertise, contacts or money that counts. While it may be true that many drug traffickers have triad connections, triad membership itself does not enhance one's position in drug organizations. The same applies to other organized crime syndicates who specialize in such activities as loan-sharking, human smuggling, credit card fraud and counterfeiting. Therefore, it should not be assumed that when a 14K triad member is arrested for a drug offence that it is the work of the Triad Society.[81]

Another major criminal enterprise historically for the Triads is narcotics smuggling. Heroin trafficking has been particularly major factor in Triad involvement in North America. In a senate hearing in 1877 on Chinese immigration, American government and law enforcement officials testified that San Francisco Chinatown was festered with opium dens which were legal at the time.[82] Although little is known about the role of Chinese traffickers in the heroin trade between the years of 1914 to 1965, it is often theorized by experts that after the liberalization of immigration laws in 1965, many Chinese criminals brought heroin into America by ship. These

---

[78] Bolz, 150.
[79] Bolz, 150.
[80] Zhang and Chin, 472.
[81] Zhang and Chin, 472.
[82] Zhang and Chin, 473.

sailors then gave the smuggled heroin to drug dealers in Chinatown who then disseminated the heroin to drug dealers in other ethnic groups.[83]

As mentioned previously, the Golden Triangle in Southeast Asia is the heroin epicenter for the Triads. Located in the northern Shan state of Burma, the Golden Triangle encompasses approximately 150,000-square miles of land.[84] The Golden Triangle is the second largest opium producing area in the world, trailing only Afghanistan. Many of the world's drug products originated here, including the methamphetamine production sites of the "speed" epidemic that plagued Thailand in the 1990s.[85]

There are several key factors why Burma has become such a vital part of the international narcotics trade and a Triad stronghold. Burma gained its independence in 1948 from the United Kingdom and the Communist Party of Burma controlled the Golden Triangle in the wake of the power vacuum left by the British. But as Communist rule weakened throughout the world (collapse of the Berlin Wall), the leaders of the Wa ethnic group in Burma separated themselves from the Communist Party of Burma and signed a deal with the central Burmese government.[86] As a result of this deal, Wa soldiers were given control of the Golden Triangle, leaving the Burmese army to focus on destroying the various rebellious democratic movements throughout the country.[87] This freedom of movement made the Wa army one of the largest and most powerful heroin trafficking groups in the world. Its men participated in all aspects of the drug business, including cultivation, production and distribution. Under the Wa, opium was legally cultivated and a prime source of tax money for the Wa army. Farmers in the area are forced to pay a tax on the opium whether or not they actually grow the crop.[88] This tax sets up a system where it incentives the farmers to grow their own poppies or buy opium in order to pay the tax. Although factories that produce these drugs are "illegal," they nevertheless operate under the informal protection of the Wa army.

Starting in the early 1990s, trade accelerated between Burma and Mainland China. Businessmen hailing from China came into the Wa controlled Golden Triangle and Burma seeking tantalizing new money-making schemes. As the Chinese came, heroin production accelerated. China's sophisticated chemical industry gave the Wa an easy and efficient access to the raw chemical materials needed for narcotics production. Once the narcotics were completed, they were shipped into China and other parts of the world.[89] Meth production skyrocketed when Thailand cracked down on their own indigenous operations in the mid-1990s. Sensing that there

---

[83] Zhang and Chin, 473.

[84] Federico Varese, *The Future of the Mafias? Foreign Triads in China* (Mafias on the Move: How Organized Crime Conquers New Territories, Princeton University Press, 2011), 172.

[85] Varese, 173.

[86] Varese, 173.

[87] Varese, 173.

[88] Varese, 173.

[89] Varese, 173.

was money to be made, Chinese Triads took advantage of the Thailand situation and accelerated their meth production in the Golden Triangle.

In order to reach China, heroin must be smuggled through the Golden Triangle into the Southern Chinese province of Yunnan and then to Guangdong, Shenzhen and Hong Kong and eventually to North America.[90] This drug trade expanded greatly in the 1990s, with law enforcement making historic drug seizures during this time. The U.S. Drug Enforcement Administration considered the Yunnan province to be the main transit point for Golden Triangle heroin in 2002.[91] From Yunnan, the drugs are then smuggled to Guangdong, which served as the primary distribution center for both the Chinese and international market. These operations are immense. In 2002, Chinese police in Guangdong seized 1,618.72 kilograms of drugs and 5,475 drug-related criminal activities.[92]

Guangdong served as the center of international drug distribution for the Chinese Triads. In Guangdong, Triads smuggled drugs into America through the port cities of Shenzhen and Hong Kong. The Triads were also constantly using different tactics to counter law enforcement detection. In the late 1980s, the Triads changed their export methods. Instead of using drug couriers who traveled to American airports from Hong Kong and Bangkok, Triad traffickers sent significant amounts of heroin (50 to 100 pounds) to ports in Newark and Elizabeth in New Jersey and Chicago.[93] These packages of heroin were placed in cargo shipping containers traveling from Shenzhen and Hong Kong. Narcotics were hidden in furniture and frozen seafood. For example, one particular incident had Triad traffickers hiding heroin in five boxes of live goldfish destined for the San Francisco aquarium.[94]

Although the Triads are intricately connected to the heroin business in Asia, many of the actual traders responsible for importing the drugs from Burma into China and around the world are actually ethnic Chinese businessmen.[95] As legitimate businessmen, these individuals can take advantage of their business connections and legal commercial operations to smuggle drugs. Many of the biggest traffickers are Chinese entrepreneurs with personal or business links to the very communities where drugs are destined to arrive.[96] As China and Burma increases their trade relationship, Chinese investors (mostly from Yunnan and Sichuan provinces) have traveled to the Wa area of Burma in increasing numbers. Because of these private Chinese business ventures, the Chinese business have been able to transport heroin without the need of Triad connections.

After 1983, Southeast Asian heroin entering the United States increased exponentially. Law enforcement believed that Chinese drug smugglers were responsible for 20 percent of the heroin

---

[90] Varese, 173.
[91] Varese, 175.
[92] Varese, 175.
[93] Varese, 175.
[94] Varese, 175.
[95] Varese, 175.
[96] Varese, 175.

imported into America.[97] In New York City in 1984, American law enforcement believed Southeast Asian heroin composed approximately 40 percent of the total heroin available in the city. However, these numbers increased rapidly. In 1990, 45 percent of heroin in America and 80 percent of heroin in New York City was Southeast Asian origin. Chinese Triads were the primary criminal groups responsible for this growth. Chinese drug dealers also worked with non-Asian criminal groups, often assisting Hispanic dealers and distributors in New York City.[98]

Gambling and Debt Collection in Macau and China

Gambling has been a major criminal enterprise for the Triads. Of particular importance is the city of Macau. A former Portuguese colony located in southern China, the city is home to the largest gambling economy in the world (surpassing Las Vegas). This booming industry has attracted a sea of loan sharks, debt collection and dispute services that perfectly align with Triad business expertise.

Since Chinese Chairman Deng Xiaoping's policies opened China to the global market economy in the 1980s, vast amounts of people have traveled to Macau. The former Portuguese colony was handed back to mainland China in 1999 and subsequently classified as a special administrative region in the People's Republic of China.[99] In 2005 alone, 10.5 million mainland Chinese visited Macau, representing a 147 percent increase from just three year earlier. In a power move to secure Macau as the gambling capital of Asia, China forced the Burmese government to shut down eighty casinos on the southern border of China.[100]

Gambling does exist in mainland China. But its presence is limited to underground gambling dens. In May 2006, Chinese state media reported that there were one hundred underground casinos in Lian ping of Guangdong Province, a massive amount considering the size of the small county.[101] Lian ping casinos were highly popular with gamblers throughout southern China, attracting people from all over. According to Guangdong police, 1,800 underground lottery outlets and casinos were raided in 2003.[102]

But Macau remains the crown jewel of the gambling world in China. Macau is home to vast sums of gambling revenue. The average table in Macau earn three times more than the equivalent table in Las Vegas.[103] Although the 2008 financial crisis hurt profits in Asia's gambling city (along with Beijing tightening visa regulations for mainland Chinese visitors). However, by summer of 2009, Macau had already recovered. Business accelerated, surpassing previous numbers.

---

[97] Zhang and Chin, 473.
[98] Zhang and Chin, 474.
[99] Varese, 163.
[100] Varese, 163.
[101] Varese, 163.
[102] Varese, 163.
[103] Varese, 163.

With gambling, comes the rise in loan sharking. And with loan sharks, come the Triads. According to official records, loan sharking accounts for the second-highest number of arrests, surpassed only by drug crimes in Macau. Frequently violent in nature, kidnapping for the purpose of collecting gambling debts has increased (24 cases in 2005 to 48 cases in 2006).[104] Diamantino Santos, a coordinator from the Macau Security Bureau, states that: "95 percent of these cases in Macau are usually related to gambling linked crimes, like loan sharking."[105]

The Triads consider collecting gambling debts a significant business. This can even lead to Triads working with other Triads to capture debt ridden Chinese gamblers. For example, the Foshan Water Room gang based in Foshan in Guangdong in mainland China formed an alliance with the Macau Sui Fong Triad (primary Triad group in Macau).[106] Together, the two groups of gangsters tracked down the families of mainland gamblers who had escaped debts. The two groups even worked together in various loan shark and sports betting schemes. Many Hong Kong Triad groups had significant influence in China for debt collection, even establishing "action teams in the mainland to collect gambling debts."[107] As stated by one police official in the Zhuhai Bureau, a few kilometers north of Macau:

There are four main [triads] groups in Macau, 14K, Water Gang, Great Ring Gang, and Wo Shing Yee. All the four main groups were discovered in Zhuhai. Their main businesses included collecting debts for Macau casinos, organizing prostitution, smuggling, kidnapping, manufacturing and selling counterfeit money and collecting protection fees. . . . [I]t was common that Macau mafias came to Zhuhai and other cities in Guangdong to recruit local members, or forge alliances with local gangs to commit crimes. This was a strategy to extend their territory of influence. For example, Wo Shing Yee of Macau established a gang in Jiangmen city [a city some one hundred kilometers northwest of Zhuhai] and provided financial support for the gang to conduct business in the mainland. But the gangsters were local thugs.[108]

The 14K Triad based in both Hong Kong and Macau are particularly ruthless in its debt collection operations. An example of these 14K operations can be illustrated by the activities of "Four-Eyed Xiong" Chen and his brother "Big Jie."[109] Allied with other gangsters, the two men tracked down gamblers with unpaid debts in mainland China. After the money was repaid, it was transferred to Hong Kong and Macau through a series of underground banks and legitimate businesses. Their methods can be illustrated by the following operation:

For instance, on the afternoon of November 18, 1996, Big Jie, Jiang, and Zeng went to the China Grand Hotel in Guangzhou to demand the repayment of HK$2.6 million from a gambler

---

[104] Varese, 164.

[105] Varese, 164.

[106] Varese, 166.

[107] Varese, 167.

[108] Varese, 167.

[109] Varese, 167.

who had borrowed money in a VIP room in Macau and failed to pay it back. Violence ensued, and one person was severely wounded. In another case, in November 1998, the general manager of the Yushun Company of Shanghai borrowed HK$300,000 from the 14K while at the gambling table of the New Century Casino in Macau. The Chen brothers demanded the repayment of this debt several times, but the manager did not return the money. In March 1999 they dispatched their team to Shanghai, where they ultimately killed the gambler's girlfriend.[110]

Triad Violence

Like many organized criminal groups, the Triads used violence as a key feature. Unlike the Italian Mafia or Japanese yakuza, Chinese Triads are not strict hierarchical command structures. Some crime experts have argued that organized crime groups centralize their power via "control and command."[111] But Chinese Triads operate as franchises, with members coordinating their group's operations away from central approval (although they are required to pay dues for their affiliation). The way the command and organization of a criminal group is important for the way it can control the implementation of violence amongst its members. Organized crime groups will generally seek to use violence as a tool, often with a rational goal in mind and for profit inducing reasons.[112] However, "brotherhoods" may seek to use violence for more emotional reasons, such as for honor or status. Some groups may adhere to a combination, using a "range of violence perhaps of a hybrid (motive) nature but centered on contract violation."[113] According to some organized experts, this can be seen in the Sicilian Mafia, where gangsters weren't just criminal entrepreneurs dealing in illegal goods but also in selling protection. This concept of protection was a commodity that was a valuable part of "economic exchange by ensuring that an illicit or licit business deal was undertaken in the absence of legal enforcement."[114]

Therefore violence was not used only for the enforcement of illegal deals and discipline but also as competition between the different criminal groups in order to gain the reputation necessary to provide this protection in society.[115] But the most sustainable criminal organizations are also careful in its use of selective violence. According to the Institute for Regional Security: "criminal associations that specialized in the distribution of illicit goods and services were more durable than those based on violence and that (irrationally) sought to monopolizes illicit markets: the latter ultimately disrupted the markets and shortened their own existence."[116]

Triad groups use much of their violence as a "brand." This brand is used primarily by the street-level Triad proxy gangs who used violence as a means of enforcing and providing protection services for various businesses (legal or illegal). Running illicit markets required a

---

[110] Varese, 168.
[111] Broadhurst and Lee, 18.
[112] Broadhurst and Lee, 18.
[113] Broadhurst and Lee, 19.
[114] Broadhurst and Lee, 19.
[115] Broadhurst and Lee, 19.
[116] Broadhurst and Lee, 19.

reputation by these street gangs "a readiness to publicize the violence–violence was essential to enforce contracts and discipline and to eliminate competitors."[117] Violence was also not strictly between protection over the various illegal trades and territory disputes, it also consisted of on subjects of honor and discipline.

In matters of honor, the Triads occupy an existence where it is not strictly a profit minded criminal organization. Triad culture includes aspects like "secrecy, loyalty and brotherhood, and 'righteousness.'"[118] These elements are actually critical to the success of discipline within the Triads.

Although a large percentage of the violence in Hong Kong is connected to the Triads, overall lethal violence appears to be decreasing. Homicide rates have been steadily declining since the early 1990s. In 1997, a quarter of homicide victims were connected to Triad violence. However, by 2001, Triad connected murders were less than one in twenty of the total number of homicides in Hong Kong. Historically, although Hong Kong has been a relatively safe city, the proportion of homicides related to Triad violence has been high. Twelve percent of homicides between 1989 to 1998, consisting of 504 offenders were Triad related.[119] Compare these numbers to the years of 1999 to 2005, where Triad-related murders were 4.9 percent of homicide cases (a significant drop from 12 percent). Triad members by virtue of their chosen profession, were thirteen times more likely to be murdered when compared to a civilian.[120]

By 2005, the homicide rate, including Triad crime, had decreased throughout Hong Kong. The majority of the violence was perpetuated by the street level gangs during street-level drug dealing and protection rackets. The largest amount of lethal incidents, about 49.5 percent, happened between the lower ranked Triad members during street crime activities. These violent acts ranged from contests of honor to disputes over territory.[121] The next section of violence, 21.1 percent, occurred between rival entrepreneurs in various enterprises. 16.8 percent of violence acts were attributed to the enforcement of goods and services due unpaid debts. Interestingly, internal discipline within Triad members was less common (13.8 percent). These internal disciplinary actions happened on both the street and network level of the Triads. Because of Hong Kong's strict gun laws, use of firearms were rare (only 9.7 percent, 12 victims between the years of 1989-1998).[122]

The Triads Evolve

Just like private corporations, organized criminal groups must evolve to avoid extinction. The

---

[117] Broadhurst and Lee, 19.
[118] Broadhurst and Lee, 19.
[119] Broadhurst and Lee, 21.
[120] Broadhurst and Lee, 22.
[121] Broadhurst and Lee, 22.
[122] Broadhurst and Lee, 22.

Chinese Triads are no exception. The operations and large scale ceremonies of the Triads have morphed in the last few decades. During the 1980s, a police bust of the Triads in Hong Kong often consisted of halting the secretive Triad ceremonies. These events included the ceremony cementing the ascension of a Dragon Head, the powerful gang leaders of the Triads.[123] Shrouded in secrecy, these ceremonies would be conducted by the advisors, White Paper Fans and Straw Sandals, the subordinates, all united together to elect their leader in an underground ritual. At the height of its power, Triads could muster hundreds of foot soldiers for battles against rivals on the streets of Hong Kong.

However, much has changed since the 1980s for the Triads and the groups have evolved to change with Hong Kong's economic development and relatively safe social society. The modern Triads are now active participants in "softer crimes."[124] Because of Hong Kong's economic development, modern Triads face a unique set of challenges. As explained by Jeffery Herbert, former superintendent in the Hong Kong police force and co-founder of Centinel, a Hong Kong based security agency, "the triads' biggest headache is loss of manpower. Traditional recruiting areas have gone, and they've lost rickshaw boys, transportation workers, construction workers, coolies, and shampoo boys—all virtually vanished. Manpower has shifted to the more lucrative and lighter risk areas. No triad wants his men locked up for 25 years now."[125]

But Triads are highly adaptive groups, its flexibility honed to a sharpness since its origins as secret societies in the Qing Dynasty. After World War Two and the rise of Communist China, the mainland was poor and chaotic. British ran Hong Kong was the gleaming pearl of China–safe and stable. Hong Kong based Triads quickly made the city the capital of organized crime in China. This made Triad recruitment a relatively easy affair, since it had a virtually endless supply of disenfranchised youth to draw members from. Many of these youth came from mainland China where social services were not as robust in Hong Kong during this time period. This meant that the Triads were able to tap into a need for services not met by legal entities.[126] There was a severe lack of housing, transportation and education as the economy was strained during the postwar era. This met many youth found the Triads as an attractive alternative career track. But as Hong Kong modernized and developed, the Triads were slowly drained of these disenfranchised youth manpower.

Hong Kong also erected Anti-Triad laws that made the gangster initiation ceremonies illegal. Therefore, modern Triads have been forced to adapt by abandoning their traditional family-style hierarchy. Modern Triad structure is now more decentralized than ever before. Triad members and foot soldiers keep in communication mostly through chat apps, like any modern member of Hong Kong society.[127] Gangsters rarely conduct in-person meetings. Because of the

---

[123] Justin Heifetz, *How to Track a Triad* (Vice, 5 Feb. 2017), 1.
[124] Heifetz, 1.
[125] Heifetz, 1.
[126] Heifetz, 2.
[127] Heifetz, 2.

abandonment of the traditional ranking system, Triad ranks are now more streamlined. Under this new linear ranking system, known as the "protector" system, gangsters are now assigned a protector, who is also themselves assigned a grand protector, who has great-grand protector and so forth. A sign of the modern internet era, Triads are also having trouble recruiting youth. The acceleration of internet gaming and social media has caused many disenfranchised youth to shelter themselves at home. This is quite different in comparison to the past when young delinquents left the house, socializing on the streets where they could fall victim to Triad recruiters.[128]

Even the nature of Triad illegal operations have seen significant changes. From the 1970s to the 1990s, Triads were heavily involved in the firearms trade in Hong Kong and throughout Asia. Triads were also major players in the illegal silver coin trade out of mainland China. As mentioned previously, Triads have been powerful traders in the narcotics market, making the groups huge sums of money in past decades. However, the narcotics market is downsizing for the Triads. Mexico's powerful Sinaloa drug cartel has now taken the majority of Hong Kong's cocaine trade. For heroin, a tiny amount, only 0.5 percent of Hong Kong's population are now users.[129] Triads are now highly risk averse to the harsh penalties of the heroin trade for low profit margins. Prostitution is another historically large component of the Triad money making empire. As Hong Kong's pimps, the gangsters ran sex rings and served as agents for prostitutes, even going so far as to practice "shi gong," which entailed a gangster testing a girl's "quality" before initiating her as a sex worker.[130] But similar to other criminal enterprises, the changing landscapes in technology has morphed the sex industry. Since the 2000s, the sex industry has been severely limited as a revenue stream for the Triads. Tech savvy young women can now use chat apps and internet to run themselves as independent sex workers. This left the Triad's traditional role as middlemen for sex work obsolete.

All these changes have manifested in Triad investment in a highly unusual industry–seafood. Hong Kong has a seemingly endless appetite for seafood. Unlike other industries (guns, drugs, prostitution), the Hong Kong government has done little to legalize against this new Triad business venture. The Triads now smuggle thousands of fish from international waters without clearing through customs.[131] Because the Triads possess existing smuggling networks and connections, shifting to seafood has been a relatively smooth affair. Hebert of Centinel states: "Hong Kong triads have existed for a long time and have established smuggling routes—the Chinese community works on connections and someone always knows someone."[132] This illegal fishing is having dramatic effects on the world's fish populations. According to Yvonne Sadovy, a professor at the University of Hong Kong, this illicit fishing has had a particular effect on

---

[128] Heifetz, 2.
[129] Heifetz, 2.
[130] Heifetz, 2.
[131] Heifetz, 3.
[132] Heifetz, 3.

Napoleon fish. One of Hong Kong's most beloved seafood species, the Napoleon fish is found in the waters around the Philippines and Indonesia. Because of the fish's habitat in these waters, the fish must be declared through legal customs. But in 2015, Sadovy estimates at least 1,000 Napoleon fish were swimming around in live fish shops in the city despite there being no official import record of any legal Napoleon fish.[133] In Sadovy's research, she's discovered that many fishing vessels don't report their live cargo because there's no legal requirement from the Hong Kong government. Therefore, "with Hong Kong fishing vessels, there's a big black hole."[134]

Another loophole discovered by Sadovy's research is that the Triads have established large fish pens in the ocean. The fishing ships that work for the Triads take their illegal catches and deposit them into these open-water pens.[135] Since these pens are located outside government-designated zones for fishing, the smugglers can hide huge amounts of fish in these pens. If the market demands more fish, the smugglers simply take their vessels to these open ocean fishery pens and take what they need. Because the government requires permits to sell at wholesale fish markets, the Triads can avoid these by keeping their catches in pens. Herbert explains: "we know that fish is brought in illegally by boat and not being delivered to fish markets, but kept in pens in Hong Kong waters. In the 80s, the government banned landing and selling [fish], except at fish markets—then fish markets brought in controls to attempt to break triad manipulation."[136] Although the Hong Kong government has made it a requirement to have sales permits at fish market, this has been ineffective at combating the Triad fish industry. Sadovy states: "I don't even know to what extent Hong Kong's fishing vessels are legal. We can't find the ownership—it's a secret trade altogether. "Are these companies paying taxes? There are no records on what the import volumes are. No one seems to know what they're doing."[137]

The Triads also ship their illegal seafood into mainland China. Although the Chinese government is enforcing these incidents, as demonstrated by their crackdown on Australia illegally exporting ½ billion worth of rock lobster to Shanghai from Hong Kong. But this is still just a fraction of the Triad's illegal seafood trade. Herbert states that the Triads are still "exploiting seafood in many areas of the world—this may range from illegal gathering to legal import to a hub [Hong Kong], and then it's smuggled into another country."[138]

Why hasn't the Hong Kong government done more to enforce stricter regulations? This is especially puzzling since the Triads have become so reliant on the seafood trade for revenue. Currently, the government seems to perceive this illegal seafood trade as a low priority. "It's too difficult, and the government wants to keep a good relationship with the traders," Sadovy states. Also experts believe this inaction is possibly rooted in Hong Kong culture's relative lack of

---

[133] Heifetz, 3.
[134] Heifetz, 3.
[135] Heifetz, 4.
[136] Heifetz, 4.
[137] Heifetz, 4.
[138] Heifetz, 5.

concern for natural conservation. Despite the obvious presence of Napoleon fish in the Hong Kong fish markets in 2015, the Hong Kong Customs and Excise Department had no explanation as to why they allowed fishing ships carrying live cargo to be exempt from declaring their volumes. An official from the department stated: "Hong Kong Customs conducts checks on passengers, cargoes, postal packets, and conveyances at various entry and exit control points and sea boundary using a risk management approach and through intelligence exchange and joint operations with local and overseas counterparts to prevent and detect illegal importation and exportation of any items which are prohibited or regulated by laws of the Hong Kong Special Administrative Region."[139]

The Triads have also entered cyberspace, reaping illicit profits through new clever digital tactics. The gangsters have taken a particular interest in e-commerce, specifically the website Taobao (along with American sites like eBay and Amazon). The Triads use these websites to sell counterfeit products.[140] As Herbert explains: "basic stuff like selling fakes on the internet is low key and easy to secure, so if you are caught, penalties are light. The big fakes are Chinese antiques, medicines, and clothing."[141] Triad e-commerce activity has reached such levels that the U.S. government placed Taobao on a blacklist of "notorious marketplaces" for excess sales of counterfeit products. Besides e-commerce, Triads are also hacking corporate databases in order to sell private and financial data. These sophisticated cybercrimes have forced law enforcement and private security to beef up their computer forensics capabilities to deal with this rising threat.

But despite these modern criminal methods, the Triads still operate some of their traditional criminal enterprises, many of them continuing to be street level activities. Triads smuggle cigarettes from mainland China into Hong Kong, an estimated $300 million industry. Experts estimate that one in every three cigarettes in Hong Kong can be traced to Triad smuggling operations.[142] Illegal diesel oil (red oil) is another money-making enterprise for the Triads. Smuggled in through mainland China, depots of red oil are hidden in derelict stores located in villages and empty buildings, all guarded by gangsters. The Triads are so entrenched with their systems and connections in Hong Kong that it is very difficult for authorities to stop. "Rising taxation rates worldwide is making this trade very lucrative and a challenge for all customs agencies," said Herbert.[143]

How does law enforcement stop these new Triads and their innovative criminal activities? Most experts argue that the key strategy is early intervention. Youth that are particularly susceptible to Triad recruiters should be the focus for law enforcement. Many experts advocate prioritizing work with high-risk youth in Hong Kong to cut off the Triad's source of manpower. This takes a multi-pronged approach featuring social workers, teachers and healthcare

---

[139] Heifetz, 5.
[140] Heifetz, 5.
[141] Heifetz, 5.
[142] Heifetz, 6.
[143] Heifetz, 6.

professionals. An example of this approach is Wong's organization Youth Carenet. Founded in 1999, Youth Carenet is a residential rehabilitation program for at-risk youth, especially those with drug abuse issues.

As technology and society changes, the Triads will continue to evolve its operations and culture. An organization with centuries of violent and business expertise, regime change and economic shifts, the Chinese Triads are an extremely clever and adaptive entity. For anti-Triad organizations like Centinel and law enforcement around the world, the mission to defeat the Triads will continue to change as it strategizes new ways to defeat the underground criminal powerhouse. Old school methods like cracking down on initiation ceremonies are no longer successful for Hong Kong police. But despite these changes, Wong states that one element will always remain constant: "fighting triad crime is like a chess game—your purpose is to win."[144]

Online Resources

<u>Other books about the Triads on Amazon</u>

Bibliography

Antony, J. Robert. "The Structures of Crime." Unruly People: Crime, Community, and State in Late Imperial South China, 1st ed., Hong Kong University Press, Hong Kong, 2016, pp. 105–125.

Bolz, Jennifer. "Chinese Organized Crime and Illegal Alien Trafficking: Humans as a Commodity." Asian Affairs, vol. 22, no. 3, 1995, pp. 147–158.

Broadhurst, Roderic, and Lee King Wa. "The Transformation of Triad 'Dark Societies' in Hong Kong: The Impact of Law Enforcement, Socio-Economic and Political Change." Security Challenges, vol. 5, no. 4, 2009, pp. 1–38.

Chen, An. "Secret Societies and Organized Crime in Contemporary China." Modern Asian Studies, vol. 39, no. 1, 2005, pp. 77–107.

Ellis, R. Evan. "Chinese Organized Crime in Latin America." PRISM, vol. 4, no. 1, 2012, pp. 64–77.

Gaylord, Mark S., et al. Introduction to Crime, Law and Justice in Hong Kong. Hong Kong University Press, HKU, 2009.

Heifetz, Justin. "How to Track a Triad." Vice, 5 Feb. 2017, www.vice.com/en_us/article/d7xxdj/how-to-track-a-triad.

---

[144] Heifetz, 6.

Lo, T. Wing. "Beyond Social Capital: Triad Organized Crime in Hong Kong and China." The British Journal of Criminology, vol. 50, no. 5, 2010, pp. 851–872.

Murray, Dian H., and Baoqi Qin. "The Origins of the Tiandihui: the Chinese Triads in Legend and History." Stanford University Press, 1994.

Overholt, Alison. "Vanishing Borders: The Expansion of Asian Organized Crime." Harvard International Review, vol. 17, no. 2, 1995, pp. 42–43.

Ownby, David. "Recent Chinese Scholarship on the History of Chinese Secret Societies." Late Imperial China, vol. 22 no. 1, 2001, p. 139-158.

Pearson, Geoffrey. "Introduction: Crime and Criminology in China." The British Journal of Criminology, vol. 42, no. 2, 2002, pp. 235–239.

Tracy, Sharon. "The Evolution of the Hong Kong Triads/Tongs into the Current Drug Market." Journal of Third World Studies, vol. 10, no. 1, 1993, pp. 22–36.

Trocki, Carl A. "The Underside of Overseas Chinese Society in Southeast Asia." The Hidden History of Crime, Corruption, and States, edited by Renate Bridenthal, 1st ed., Berghahn Books, 2013, pp. 149–170.

Varese, Federico. "The Future of the Mafias? Foreign Triads in China." Mafias on the Move: How Organized Crime Conquers New Territories, Princeton University Press, 2011, pp. 146–187.

Zhang, Sheldon and Ko-lin Chin. "The Declining Significance of Triad Societies in Transnational Illegal Activities: A Structural Deficiency Perspective." The British Journal of Criminology, vol. 43, no. 3, 2003, pp. 469–488.

Free Books by Charles River Editors

We have brand new titles available for free most days of the week. To see which of our titles are currently free, <u>click on this link</u>.

Discounted Books by Charles River Editors

We have titles at a discount price of just 99 cents everyday. To see which of our titles are currently 99 cents, <u>click on this link</u>.

Made in the USA
Las Vegas, NV
17 October 2023

79255734R00020